REVIEWS FOR:

Royalty

This book is amazing. It made me feel as if I was having a cup of coffee with my very best friend. I love how you instantly dive in bringing the reader close to you, allowing us to instantly feel the love of a Savior who desires to meet us right where we are. Annie is an OVERCOMER!!!! You came out the big gate letting us know that.

I can appreciate that. Oftentimes in books, we have to wait for a happy ending, here you start letting us know miracles are the norm for those who believe. Thank you for reminding us as women not to neglect our first love, which is our relationship with Christ. The scripture references, the consistent reference to prayer and atonement all make for a VERY relatable, easy to follow, devotional that I can imagine would accompany MANY purses. I had a vision of women reading this in waiting rooms, in-car lines. You speak to each woman; the corporate success mogul who is struggling in her walk AND the mama trying to just make it with her babies and the Lord. I cannot WAIT to hear the testimonies that pour in.

—**Stephanie Byrd**, Christian Comedian, Speaker, and CEO of *Personified Greatness*.

***

Royalty, speaks to women of all ages and walks of life. Whether or not we have experienced any of these circum-

stances we can all relate to them in our lives. The transp‐
ency shared drew you in to a Savior who is present and n‐
in every circumstance. It reminds all women that nothing
too hard for God.

— **Theresa Williamson**, Leader, Teacher at *Church of*
Highlands.

***

I truly believe that the women who will read this resour
and apply its truths will definitely be blessed with a grea
knowledge of their identity in Christ. Your content is ve
rich, thought-provoking and beautifully written.

—**Pastor Courtney J. Winston**, *Church of the Highlands*

Royalty

Women in Purpose

Annie Betts

Dedication

I dedicate this this book to my loving daughters, Kristian and Chloé, and to all women across the globe.

Women are life bearers. We carry life, whether physical or spiritual. We were built to care for people and things in a special way. There was one time in the Bible when God-said something wasn't good, and that was when He told Adam in Genesis 2:18, that it was not good for man to be alone. God said, "I will make a helper who is just right for him." I believe that we are not only created to help man, but also to help mankind. To show and display God's strength, love and purpose, I want my daughters to know that as long as they keep God first, they will continue to be strong enough and bold enough to be exactly who God says they are.

Daughters of God, help bring Heaven to earth, birth nations both spiritually and physically, and make Hell tremble through your love for Jesus. You are Royalty; you were built to breathe life and hope of a resurrected King in the earth.

TABLE OF CONTENTS

Introduction

Homeless. As I stood there listening to a family member try to console and encourage me, those words rang out like a siren to my heart, "You're homeless." Staring into thin air, I felt like I was a failure. I had lost everything. Those words sank deep and penetrated old wounds, making them feel fresh again. Those two words seemed to undo all the progress I had made in my faith journey. In that moment, I did not feel like a child of God.

I felt ashamed, unworthy, and hopeless. Those two simples, yet powerful, words were sent out without a thought, but aimed to kill, steal, and destroy every ounce of hope, and strength that I thought I'd built up over the years. Those words rekindled old flames of worry and insecurity. Those words echoed the mistakes of my past and tried to convince me that "Homeless" was now my name because we lost our home. Those flames of worry, insecurity, shame, and guilt were about to burn my faith and my family to the ground.

Why did standing there hearing those words feel so familiar? Why did all of this feel so familiar?

You see, the voice of our failures is familiar; it echoes our past mistakes, tells us we're not doing enough, and that we're not good enough. The familiar voice of failure tells us it will never get any better, and we're destined to repeat our past over and over. Sometimes, it can feel like our trials are on repeat, with no end in sight.

I see now that when I began this journey with Jesus, I must have naively thought being a Christian meant that life would be trouble-free. I was thinking that the problems I would face, if any, would be minor, like traffic on the way to work, or running out of gas because I thought I could drive five more miles on "E." *Don't judge me.*

But seriously, the truth is, it can be easy to underestimate the things that humble us the most.

> Isaiah 54:17 says *"No weapon formed against you shall prosper, and every tongue which rises up against you in judgment, you shall condemn. This is the heritage of the servants of the Lord..."*

The verse doesn't say the weapon won't form, it says that it won't prosper. But what do we do when we're face-to-face with the weapon? What do we do when we don't feel so powerful, or so fearless?

When quitting is not an option and running is out of the question, how do we silence the familiar voice of false accusations and failure?

In this book, we dive into the source of our feelings of defeat. We will learn practical ways found in the Word of God to get some grit, look our fear in the face, and tell it to kick rocks. When life gets overwhelming and you don't have time to catch your breath between trials, I believe that God has a right now Word for each of us! He has something to say about who you are. He has some promises for you and me that will equip and empower us to no longer listen to the lies of unworthiness, but to walk like the Royal women we are.

Chapter 1

Progress through Pain

Would I ever bring this nation to the point of birth and then not deliver it? asks the Lord. "*No! I would never keep this nation from being born,*" *says your God.* **Isaiah 66:9**

God has a way of using painful experiences in our lives to birth miracles. When we look throughout Scripture, we see many times when God used a situation that seemed painful and hopeless to bring forth new life and new beginnings. Just look at the story of the birth of our Savior Jesus Christ. Even though Mary went through the pain of childbirth, she had the privilege of birthing a living, breathing miracle who would save all mankind and restore them back to their Heavenly Father.

There are many accounts in Scripture such as with Moses, Abraham, Joseph, and Paul—who all went through different trials. They knew what it was like to go through a process of pain before a life-altering, world-changing miracle would be birthed.

When I was pregnant with my first child, I was scared to death. Here I was about to be responsible for another person's life, and I had no idea what that meant. I was still a kid myself. I came home from college and I would cry in my room every night. I was scared, confused, ashamed, and desperately needed direction. *I was afraid to be a single mother.* I had watched how hard it was for my mom to be a single mom raising me and my brothers. And there I was, about to walk in the same footsteps. I didn't want to let my mom down, and what would I say when I called my dad? I didn't want to let anyone down, but most of all, I didn't want to let down this beautiful baby boy who hadn't even gotten here yet.

My older brother came into my room one evening and handed me this prayer written on a piece of paper. The prayer was to accept Jesus Christ in my heart. All he said was, "Just read this. This is all you need." I thought, *What!? This prayer? How could this help me? How is this prayer supposed to give me direction?* I threw the prayer on my dresser and sarcastically grumbled to my brother, "Okay, sure."

As time went by, I still felt a void. This beautiful being was growing inside of me day by day, and I knew I needed help in order to give this young man a good head start in this life. I just didn't know what that would look like. Getting ready for work one morning, I glanced at the dresser where I had laid down the prayer my brother had given me. I felt like I was being drawn to this paper with the prayer written on it. I picked it up and stared at it. Although I desperately wanted the pain, the heartache, and the worry to go away, I was still doubtful. *What does my brother know anyway? He doesn't know what I need; let's just see if this prayer "works," then he'll see that a piece of paper can't fix anything.* I began to repeat the prayer out loud. When I was done, I felt a peace come over me. I started that prayer as one person, but when I was done, I was a different person. I had been transformed from the inside out. It's hard to put into words. My circumstance didn't change, but I wasn't afraid anymore. I didn't feel the weight of worry and hurt that I had been carrying. From that moment on, all the anxiety and confusion I had felt on the inside was replaced with this beautiful, sweet peace.

In the days following, this 18-year-old girl was drastically being changed from the inside out. Each day, I felt a drawing to get up at 4 AM. And I was NOT a morning person! I was more of a "don't breathe in my direction until after I drank 5 cups of coffee" type of person. But seriously, all of a sudden, I had this desire to wake up early. Back then, there was nothing on tv at 4 AM except white noise and a few infomercials. But there was one tv station that had pastors preaching, so I would sit there, wide awake watching the sermons on tv. There was one pastor at that time who seemed to be speaking directly to me. I would sit there thinking, *What? Wait, how did he know that? He don't know my life!*, not realizing that God was using this pastor to speak to me. I would follow along with his teachings in the Bible and he seemed to make my King James Version Bible make sense.

Nine months seemed to fly by, and soon my beautiful baby boy was on the scene. But do you know that when you are in a season of birthing a miracle, the enemy is waiting for you to quit prematurely? 1 Peter 5:8 (NLT) says, "Stay alert. Watch out, for your great enemy, the devil, prowls around like a roaring lion, looking for someone to devour." I had a lot of other circumstances and life-threatening events that threatened to kill me and this amazing new human being, and all I can say is, BUT GOD! What should have been a day of celebration and rejoicing at the birth of this baby, turned out to be a day full of drama. We were

3

surrounded by people who did not want this sweet boy to enter this world. That day was filled with dozens of phone calls to my hospital room from people threatening to kill my son and me.

With my mom, brother, dad, and nurses close by our side trying to protect us, this 18-year-old new mom was afraid. I wanted to know, *where was God? Will He protect us?* I stayed a week in the hospital where my son and I had to be moved to a secure room, guarded by security officers due to the violent threats.

During that week, my blood pressure had gotten severely high, and I was having symptoms of a mild stroke. I could not walk, and I had trouble speaking and understanding. My mom stayed by my side, helping to take care of my son. I was on heavy doses of magnesium through an IV, as well as being on multiple, different blood pressure medications. But nothing seemed to help lower my blood pressure. Instead, it was steadily increasing. At this point, the doctors were concerned that my heart couldn't take much more. My nurse came into my room one day and said that they would have to bring in a cardiologist because all the tests they ran were showing that my heart function was started to decrease. My body seemed to be getting weaker by the second. The day the cardiologist was on his way to the hospital to see me, he was involved in a fatal car accident and did not survive. The nurse delivered this news to my mom and told her it would be another day before another specialist could come to see me. Then the nurse whispered to my mom, "At the way things are looking from your daughter's tests, she may not make it through the night. Her heart function is decreasing and her heart is under a lot of stress." My mom cried and the nurse hugged and comforted her. My mom turned to me, with tears still in her eyes. I felt defeated and wanted to quit. This was just too much. I thought to myself, *I'm only 18 years old, how could my heart be failing?*

My mom called my brother and told him what the nurses and doctors were saying about my heart. He asked her to hold the phone to my ear so that I could hear what he was going to say next. He told me that Jesus loves me and that Jesus bore all of our sickness and sins on the cross and rose up out of the grave, victorious over death. He then began to speak the Word of God over me. He told me to speak Isaiah 53:3-5 over my body. He knew I could barely speak, but I believed that what God said in His Word is true, so I decided to do it anyway. I began mumbling those verses over and over. I wanted to live and hold my baby. I wanted to go home and love on this sweet angel. I desperately wanted God to rescue us and bless us to live a normal life free from fear. I wanted to give my son the best gift he could ever receive; I wanted to have an opportunity to share the hope of Jesus Christ with him.

As I was mumbling this verse, I started being able to slowly move my mouth more to speak clear words. Then I was able to sit up. I then turned to my mom and said, "Mom, I'm going home tomorrow." My mom just looked at me with the concerned look of a mother, and rubbed my hair and said, "Okay baby." My mom left out to go speak with one of the nurses. While she was gone, I was still declaring over my body that by the stripes of Jesus Christ I am healed and made whole. I began to slide out of the bed and struggle to stand. I hadn't been able to walk in over a week. As I looked at my son sleeping peacefully in the hospital bassinet, I attempted to walk to the bathroom. I was dragging my left leg the whole time. By now, the bathroom seemed to be a million miles away. But I kept telling God, "I believe what You say is true. I believe that you are healing me, and that I am going home tomorrow." I kept declaring Isaiah 53:3-5, and I finally made it to the bathroom, and by this time, I was not just able to slowly speak those verses, but I was shouting them out loud! With my voice trembling, I was crying, shouting, and telling the Lord that I loved Him and speaking that verse over again. In the middle of me doing this, my mom and the nurse came back into the room. I'm pretty sure I looked like a crazy person standing in the bathroom crying and loudly speaking the Word of God. But I didn't care who saw me, I didn't care who heard me. I just wanted God to hear my heart. I was desperate, and I was trusting God.

After I had stopped, the nurse helped me back into the bed. She said they would need to run more tests on me, because it seemed impossible, after an entire week of only being able to just barely speak or walk that now I was clearly speaking and walking. I told her, "That's fine, you can run more tests, but I am healed and I am going home tomorrow." She patted my arm with a look of concern and doubt and then left out to order the tests. Throughout the night, they ran many more tests, scans, and labs, and each one came back normal! My blood pressure was normal, and my body showed no signs of ever having stroke symptoms. More importantly, my newborn son and I went home the next morning!

Now, I'm not declaring that when we speak or claim God's Word that it's like waving a magic wand or performing some magic trick. But what I am saying is that just like God says in Isaiah 55:10-11, His Word does not return to Him void, it will accomplish what He sent it out to do. When we release God's Word over our lives, it accomplishes just what He says it will do; it may not always look like what we expect it to look like, but it's always for our good.

So, my sweet sister, even though the enemy may want to threaten you and surround you with suffocating circumstances, don't quit before it's time for you to birth your miracle. You can labor without fear, because "God did not give us a Spirit of fear and timidity, but of power, love and a sound mind." (2 Timothy 1:7) Your season of birthing a miracle may look like a heart-pounding, nerve-wracking pain on every side. It may feel like you're out of breath. It may feel like you're just downright exhausted by striving to make things work or to fix that problem. Maybe you're trying to fix that relationship, or just trying to make ends meet. Let me tell you, my sweet sister, don't quit. Surrender to the process. God did not cause the pain you may be experiencing now or any pain you may have gone through in the past, but He loves you and will use this season and that circumstance to birth a miracle in your life.

Jesus gave us a promise in John 16:33 saying, "Though in this life, you will have many struggles, take heart because I have overcome them all." You are not defeated, you have victory on every side. Whatever was supposed to destroy you, kill your hope, or deter you, God will turn it around for your good. You are still here, and still have breath in your body; that means that you still have purpose.

I'm believing and declaring over you right now, the same words that God declared over Israel in Isaiah 43, "But now, this is what the Lord says, He who created you, Jacob, He who formed you, Israel, 'Do not fear, for I have redeemed you; I have summoned you by name;

you are Mine. **When** <u>you pass through the waters</u>, <u>I will be</u> **with you**; and **when** <u>you pass through the riv-ers</u>, <u>they will</u> **not** <u>sweep over you</u>. **When** <u>you walk through the fire</u>, <u>you</u> **will not** <u>be burned;</u> <u>the flames</u> **will not** <u>set you ablaze</u>. For I am the Lord your God the Holy One of Israel, your Savior...'" He didn't say "<u>If</u> you go through the waters," or "<u>if</u> you go through the fire," He said, "W<u>hen</u> you do, I won't let them take you out! I'll be right there."

God has redeemed you and has called you by name. You are His daughter. Whatever you walk through in this life, He is right there with you. Not only will He guide you, but He will protect you and bring you victo-riously through that situation. So, get ready, my sister, if you are in the midst of a painful season, you are about to birth something new: a new ministry, new re-lationship, and/or new business. Put this book down for a second and shout to the Lord in praise right now! Declare over yourself that you are a new creature in Christ Jesus, and that you are birthing a new thing! Hallelujah!

I don't ever want to take for granted that everyone reading this book may already have a relationship with Jesus Christ. If you find yourself thinking, "I des-perately need peace right now," or "I just need help with this situation," or if you have this feeling that something is just missing, have you tried to fill that void, but nothing has worked so far? I want to offer an opportunity, right now, to invite Jesus Christ into your heart. This is personal, and this is just for you.

And if you're anything like how I used to be, you might be thinking to yourself, "How can this prayer help me or change my life?" I want to ask you to just try it. That's all, just try it. None of us are perfect, and at some point, we have said, done, or thought something wrong. Being a Christian does not mean living a perfect life. It means acknowledging that we are all broken and need help from a perfect Savior, Jesus Christ. The Bible says, "All have sinned and fallen short of the glory of God." (Romans 3:23) But the good news is that Jesus died in our place so we could have a relationship with God and be with Him forever (Romans 5:8). And guess what? It didn't just end with His death, Jesus rose again, and is still alive! (1 Corinthians 15:3-4)

We can't forgive our own sins or earn our way to Heaven. The only way to Heaven is through Jesus and Jesus said, "I am the way, and the truth, and the life; no one comes to the Father, but through Me." (John 14:6) The Word says, "If you declare with your mouth, 'Jesus is Lord,' and believe in your heart that God raised Him from the dead, you will be saved." (Romans 10:9)

If you are ready and willing to accept His help, and most of all, His extravagant love for you, take a moment and get by yourself, and pray something like this:

Dear God,
I know that I am a sinner, and I ask for your forgiveness.
I believe Jesus Christ is Your Son. I believe that He died for my sins and that You raised Him to life.
I want to trust Him as my Savior and follow Him as Lord from this day forward.
Guide my life and help me to do Your will.
I pray this in the name of Jesus. Amen.

If you prayed that prayer, I want you to know that all of Heaven's angels are rejoicing right now! (Luke 15:7,10)

I'm rejoicing right now with you, and praying that God leads you to a Bible-based church, where you can connect with other people who are genuinely in love with Jesus and can help you grow deeper in God's Word.

Chapter 2

Proceed with Boldness

Have I not commanded you? Be strong and courageous. Do not be afraid; do not be discouraged, for the Lord your God will be with you wherever you go. **Joshua 1:9**

After going through any type of trauma or any major change in life, it can be easy for fear to set in. Maybe it's bad news from the doctor, or rumors or concerns of a national pandemic. Fear seems to always be lurking at the door, waiting for the right opportunity to make itself at home in our hearts. Oftentimes, we're ready to answer the door to fear with questions like, "How will I handle this?" "What's next?" "What does this mean for my future, my family or career?" or "How long will this thing last?" These are all valid questions. Now don't get me wrong, fear is real and very valid. But my hope in this chapter is that we would give fear its walking papers and tell it to kick rocks and never return!

God reminds us in 2 Timothy 1:7 that "God did not give us a spirit of fear and timidity, but of power, love, and a sound mind." A sound mind is sanity in the midst of insane and impossible circumstances. A sound mind is not necessarily your situation or circumstances changing, but your heart changing in the midst of your situation.

There have been many times when I was faced with fear. To be honest, it was in the most personal areas, such as jobs, health, finances, and children. I look back on those areas now and I'm beyond grateful that when I let go, God got me through whatever it was with such peace, and better than I could have ever imagined. For about 14 years of my oldest son's life, there were many more attempts from the other side of his family to harm us, even attempts to kidnap him. But God proved to be faithful throughout each occurrence. When he went to visit them, oftentimes I would go days without sleep, worried that this time they would follow through on their threats to hurt him, or not bring him back home to me. I would wonder each time, *Will I see my son again, or will I have to go and search for my son again because they refused to give him back or tell me where he was?* I would cry and pray and worry if I would find him and he would be unharmed. *Will God bring him home safely this time?* I cannot begin to explain the fear and anxiety that would set in during those times.

Then came the season of surrender. He went to visit his family and almost a month passed, but my son was not back yet. I could barely focus to work. All the worries and fears overwhelmed me and I could not see my computer screen for the heavy stream of tears flooding my eyes. Then, I heard God say, "Look at Deuteronomy 30:4 -9." I turned to it, and through my tears began to read these words:

> *"No matter how far away you end up, God, your God, will get you out of there and bring you back to the land your ancestors once possessed. It will be yours again. He will give you a good life and make you more numerous than your ancestors. God, your God, will cut away the thick calluses on*

*your heart and your children's hearts, freeing
you to love God, your God, with your whole heart
and soul and live, really live. God, your God, will
put all these curses on your enemies who hated
you and were out to get you. And you will make
a new start, listening obediently to God, keeping
all his commandments that I'm commanding you
today. God, your God, will outdo himself in making things go well for you..."*

I began laughing through the tears. God did just
what He said: Not only did my son come back home,
but God blessed my son to be brave enough to share
the trauma that he faced each time he went to visit. My
son prayed and he wrote me a note explaining the
things that he faced, and one line that I will never forget said, "Mommy, I prayed that God would free me,
and bring me back home to stay with you and be safe."
And God did just that. God blessed my husband to
adopt my son, and since then my son has been on the
road to healing and has been growing fervently in his
relationship with Jesus.

Listen, where you are right now, woman of God, is
on purpose. God has not left you. He will not leave you.
He has not forgotten what He promised you. Even if
you have decided to leave Him, He will never leave
you. He is with you and He will do exactly what He said
He will do. You will be restored, and God will outdo
Himself in making things go well for you.

The most recent time I was faced with fear was
when I had our baby girl. I was dealing with chronic
high blood pressure again. My blood pressure at the
time was averaging around 240s/116 or higher! I
prayed day and night that I would wake up again and
get to see my sweet kiddos. But because my blood

pressure was so high for too long, my OB/ GYN made the wise but difficult decision to deliver our baby girl early at 31 weeks via emergency C-section. She only weighed 3lbs. and my blood pressure struggled to get under control.

Each day as I healed, my husband and I would go and visit our daughter in the NICU and pray over her. Each day was a step into the unknown, not knowing what the outcome would be and not knowing when it would all be okay again. We both cried each day, not only as we prayed for our daughter, but also as we were praying for healing over my body. We watched doctors and specialists come in and out my hospital room around the clock, attempting to get my blood pressure under control. I was on four different blood pressure medicine. With each headache, each new symptom, and being told that I was too young for my blood pressure to stay this high for so long and how high blood pressure is a silent killer, I prayed to God to please let me live. The fear of what happened to my health before started to creep in. I mean, it almost looked the same. I would think, *Why would this happen again?*

There's an old saying, that where the devil had success before, he will try again. Let me tell you right now that you might be facing a situation that <u>looks</u> deadly, that <u>looks</u> like your past, that <u>looks</u> like defeat, but my God, our faithful Abba Father, has other plans for you. He has victory on the other side of the unknown. The Psalmist said, "Though I walk through the valley of the **<u>shadow</u>** of death, I will fear no evil, for you are with me Lord, your rod and staff protect me." (Psalm 23)

Woman of God, that fear of death, whether it's a fear

of a dying marriage, dying finances, dying health, dying career, or dying dreams, is JUST a shadow. Our Father has you and will protect you and bring you out on top.

Although each day was unknown to us, it did not stop my husband and me from declaring God's word over our fears. Some days, with tears in my eyes and weariness in my body and soul, I would just praise God and tell Him who He is. My prayers consisted of ugly sobs and asking God, "How long?" until I finally surrendered. Then, my prayers looked more like just telling Him that I trusted Him even though it was hard. I cannot tell you how my husband was feeling, but there were many days when he stood over me with tears in his eyes, yet bold faith in his voice, pouring encouragement and God's Word over me.

I heard a pastor say one time, "We need to decide who we are letting sit on the throne. Are we letting fear, or God sit on the throne of our hearts?" That statement was powerful to me because what we worship will rule our lives.

Now, I'm not here to tell you that I have it all figured out, or that I perfectly and boldly walked through every season of hard times. There were times when I pleaded repeatedly to God and asked Him, "Where are You?" and "Did You hear me?" There were many moments of feeling so depleted that I didn't have any words to pray. But God is always right there with us. Just as Moses told Joshua in Deuteronomy 31:6, God's promise still stands true today. "Be strong and courageous. Do not fear or be in dread of them, for it is the Lord your God who goes with you. He will not leave you or forsake you."

It is the Lord who is with you, and the Lord who will

never leave you. He is not mad at you, He loves you. The same God that moved Heaven and earth to get to you through His Son Jesus, is the same God that hears your midnight cries. He is not happy about your sorrow. He is yet using every tear and every heartache to build you, and soon those tears and fears will be a testament of His faithfulness in your life.

God is going to use what you have gone through as a powerful testimony to help someone else. Wherever you are, your heart may be heavy and tired, but you are a daughter of the Most High King. No matter what you're facing, you can go through it boldly because the One and True Living God is on your side. Sing your way through this time, declare the victory of Heaven over your situation! Declare Heaven in your sorrow and make hell tremble! Because what should have broken you is about to build you. What should have shattered your faith is about to light a fire in your spirit that will move mountains.

You are not going down without a fight, woman of God, and you ain't fighting alone!

Read Joshua 1:1-9. What is God saying to you? Is there new territory where God is leading you and that fear keeps trying to keep you from entering the promise that God gave you? How will you proceed with boldness?

_____

_____

_____

_____

Chapter 3

You are Priceless!

For you created my inmost being;
you knit me together in my mother's womb.
I praise you because I am fearfully and wonder-
fully made; your works are wonderful, I know that
full well. **Psalm 139:13-14**

There are times when I used to sit and wonder, *why am I here? What's my purpose? I mean, there are billions of people on this planet, so what makes me different?* If you have ever wondered the same thing, you're not alone. One of the biggest questions most people ask on this planet, is "What's my identity?" (who they are) and "What's my purpose?" Those are two valid but huge questions.

Did you know there's an answer? When we ask those two questions in our faith community, sometimes we're met with the vague answer, "Just seek the Lord," or "Pray about it and He'll show you the answer." Well, sometimes I might be sending God the message, and when I check back for an answer, God left me on read. Am I the only one?

But God perfectly knit each one of us together in our mother's womb. <u>On purpose.</u> Not by accident, but on purpose. You were born on purpose, for a purpose. Even if your earthly parents didn't plan your birth, God did! He always knew from the beginning that the world He created, would need a YOU. And there is not another person exactly like you.

No matter where you were born, or what circumstances or family you were born into, you were created to be a chain- breaker, a generational curse ender, and a bridge to turn brokenness into healing.

Your purpose is the thing that breaks your heart the most. It's the thing that, when you hear about it, you feel this over-whelming passion deep on the inside of you, that goes beyond empathy; it makes you feel uneasy until you do something. It could be to bring more creativity, hope, or healing into the world by being an artist, a singer, a doctor, a teacher, or something completely different. What is the thing you feel you were born to be a solution for in the earth? That, my sister, is your purpose.

Sometimes, we know what breaks our hearts or we know what our purpose is, but we get discouraged or deterred by the lies of our enemy. In John 8, Jesus calls Satan the father of lies. The enemy can whisper the same lies of hopelessness to all of us. Lies like, "This is just my life, nothing will ever change," or "I can't help but be like this, my whole family is like this," or "This is who I am," or "I'm not qualified. I'm not good enough." Or maybe you just have the doubts of, "Am I really called to do that?" But God declares in Jeremiah 29:11, "For I know the plans I have for you ... plans to prosper you and not harm you, plans to give you hope and a future." The truth is, you are qualified, and yes, you are good enough.

We live in a broken world and a lot of people didn't grow up in the most ideal situations or the safest parts of town. But even if you grew up in a toxic environment, or have experienced some trauma throughout your life, know that God did not cause the trauma. If you are reading this book, that means God brought you through, or is bringing you through right now. He cares about every tear you shed and every pain you feel. He still has a plan for you. It's a plan to give you hope and a future. He will not only heal you, but He will use your experiences to heal others.

Let's look at the story of Joseph, beginning in Genesis 37. First of all, Joseph was one of 12 sons. Talk about a crowd! Joseph was born to a father (Jacob) who showed favoritism toward his sons. Because of this, there was a lot of jealousy and division among Joseph and his brothers. I wouldn't have wanted to be invited to Thanksgiving at their house!

If things weren't tense enough between Joseph and his brothers, God started giving Joseph dreams. In the dreams, Joseph's brothers and his mother and father would bow down to him. And Joseph shared these dreams with his brothers and his father.

This caused the brothers to be even more jealous. And one day, when Joseph came to check on his brothers while they were out pasturing sheep, his brothers plotted to kill Joseph.

But instead of killing him, they decided to sell him for twenty pieces of silver to a group of Ishmaelite traders. Those traders then took Joseph to Egypt, where they sold him to Potiphar, an officer of the Pharaoh, the ruler of Egypt.

Genesis 39:2, says, "The Lord was with Joseph, so he succeeded in everything he did as he served in the home of his Egyptian master." Joseph soon became Potiphar's right-hand man. Joseph was put in charge of his master's household and property. It seemed that

God was beginning to turn things around for Joseph. He went from being rejected by his own brothers and sold into slavery to being promoted to handling royal affairs.

Now, in the midst of things looking brighter for Joseph, he was still faced with a few trials that seemed to keep him from fulfilling his God-given purpose.

Have you ever felt like things were starting to look brighter and better, and here comes something that throws you a curve ball? Something that causes all of those feelings of failure, insecurity, rejection, fear, and doubt to surface again? Joseph knew a little something about that, as well. He faced being falsely accused of attempted rape by Potiphar's wife, and he was then thrown into jail. But Genesis 39:21 says, "But the Lord was with Joseph in the prison and showed him his faithful love."

You may feel like you've just made three steps forward and you started to feel hopeful again. Then here comes the accuser, our adversary the devil. The false accusations may be from people or just from your own thoughts. The accusations could be based on what it looks like: lies of being an addict, a failure, not worthy of love, being called a bad mom, a bad wife, not good enough, or not doing enough. Whatever the accusations that are spoken to you by your accuser, the devil, to put you back in bondage, know that you have been set free, and God is with you and is about to show His faithful love towards you. You see, faithful is not just what God does, it's who He is! He's faithful. He is love and He hasn't left you stranded. He doesn't call you by your mistakes. Neither does He call you by the names of your past. You are not being left bound and alone in a prison of lies. Jesus said that He came so that we would have life, and life to the full (John 10:10). It ain't over for you yet. Your story does not end here.

Looking again at the story of Joseph, we see that God began to elevate Joseph while he was in prison. Joseph was favored by the prison warden and was then put in charge of all the prisoners and over everything that happened in the prison (vs. 22). Because the Lord was with Joseph, He caused everything Joseph did to succeed (v 23).

God's purpose for you cannot be stopped or thwarted by any force of nature, or by anyone's hand. No matter what the enemy has tried to throw your way this far, or what trials you've had to overcome, God still has a plan for you. Your God-given purpose is rooted in your spirit and will grow and produce a great harvest, if you do not quit but continue to surrender to the Lord.

While Joseph was still in prison, God used Joseph to interpret the dreams of a chief cup bearer and a chief baker who had been thrown into prison with Joseph. He told the chief baker his dream meant that in three days' time, he would be put to death. Joseph told the chief cup bearer that in three days, the Pharaoh would restore him back to his position as chief cup bearer. Joseph also asked the chief cup bearer that when that happened, to mention him to Pharaoh so that he could be freed, too. The interpretations of those dreams came to pass; the chief baker was put to death and the chief cup bearer was restored back to his position. However, the chief cup bearer forgot about Joseph and failed to mention him to Pharaoh. Two years went by and Joseph was still in prison.

Sometimes, it may seem that the answers to our prayers are being delayed, that maybe God forgot us.

But a delay is not a denial.

After two years, the chief cup bearer finally remembered Joseph, after Pharaoh had a few disturbing dreams and was looking for someone to interpret them. The chief cup bearer told Pharaoh how Joseph accurately interpreted his dream, so Pharaoh gave Joseph an opportunity to interpret his dream. God used Joseph to interpret Pharaoh's dreams of a warning by God that there would be seven years of abundance followed by seven years of famine. Pharaoh was pleased with Joseph's suggestions to gather and store food during the years of abundance in order to prepare for the years of scarcity. So, Pharaoh put Joseph in charge of his court. In Genesis 41:40-41, we see that Pharaoh put Joseph in charge of all of Egypt and was second in command under Pharaoh.

Joseph went from being in bondage to being promoted above his previous position. So, don't worry about any setbacks you may have faced in this lifetime. Your setbacks will be a setup for success.

As predicted, the seven years of abundance and the years of famine came to pass in Egypt. Joseph oversaw the gathering and storing of grain during the years of abundance, as well as the distribution of grain during the years of famine. During the famine, people came from all over to get grain from Egypt, including Joseph's older brothers. Genesis 42:6 says that "since Joseph was governor of all Egypt, and in charge of selling grain to all the people, it was to him that his brothers came." The next verses go on to say how Joseph recognized his brothers instantly, but pretended to be a stranger, so they didn't recognize him.

You see, it was easy for Joseph not to be recognized, because he didn't look like what he had gone through.

I can tell you right now, without seeing you face to face, that you, daughter, do not look like what you've gone through. That God has exchanged those bumps, bruises and scratches of your past for royal clothing and a revived soul!

Joseph went through a series of events as he processed coming face-to-face with his brothers. These actions included treating them harshly, then blessing them, throwing them in jail, blessing them again, holding one brother hostage, preparing a grand feast for them, and even framing them to look like thieves. Ultimately, Joseph went through a wide range of emotions—emotions that were very much understandable. We see in several verses where he wept and then had to compose himself so that he could continue dealing with his brothers.

That must have been hard for Joseph to see his brothers after all that time, especially after all they had done to him. They threw him away. I'm sure there were feelings of bitterness, rejection, rage, and sadness. After Joseph had gone through processing his encounter with his brothers, he finally revealed to them who he really was.

His brothers felt sorry and ashamed for what they had done to Joseph, but Joseph told his brothers in Genesis 45:5, 7, not to feel bad about what they had done, because "it was God who sent him ahead of them to preserve the lives of their families." Because of Joseph's obedience to God, many people survived the famine. God had positioned him there on purpose. God did not cause the trauma that Joseph went through, but God didn't waste it either. He used every step of Joseph's journey to not only redeem Joseph, but also to save many people.

Joseph said to his brothers again in Genesis 50:20, "You intended to harm me, but God intended it all for my good. He brought me to this position so I could save the lives of many people."

Maybe, like Joseph, you know what it feels like to be rejected, to feel thrown aside by the ones who were supposed to protect you and love you. But they turned their back on you or left you vulnerable to harm, instead. I'm here to tell you that God did not intend for any of those hurtful things to happen to you. But I can assure you that God wastes nothing! He will use every step, every season, every heartache and tear, to not only redeem you, but to place you sure-footed and grounded in your purpose. When we surrender completely to the Lord, He lifts us out of the things that had us bound in rejection, shame, guilt, and insecurity. He then immerses us into our purpose that propels others towards new life.

When God gets ready to elevate you, just like Joseph, you won't look like your past. But you will be able to look your past in the face with humility and grace because it was God who brought you through. And sister, he ain't done blessing you yet!

Write Psalm 139:13-14.

_____

_____

_____

What are some things that God has brought you through? How can you use this experience to help someone who may be going through the same thing?

_____

_____

_____

_____

_____

_____

_____

_____

_____

_____

_____

_____

_____

_____

Chapter 4

Adjust Your Crown

But you are a chosen people, a royal priesthood, a holy nation, God's special possession, that you may declare the praises of Him who called you out of darkness into His wonderful light. **1 Peter 2:9**

You may have heard this verse a dozen times in church, or this may be your first time to read this verse, but did you know, daughter, that YOU are ROYALTY! That's right. You are a co-heir with Christ Jesus. When you accepted Jesus Christ as your living Savior, you also became God's daughter. You are now a part of the royal family. As long as you believe in your heart and confess with your mouth that Jesus is Lord, NOTHING, I mean absolutely NOTHING can change that.

Listen, let's look at this verse bit-by-bit. I want you to write this verse but put your name where it says "you." Like this,

But [Your Name] is a <u>chosen people</u>, a <u>royal priesthood</u>, a <u>holy nation</u>, God's <u>special possession,</u> that [Your Name] may declare the praises of him who <u>called [Your Name] out of darkness</u> into his wonderful light.

Let's put it like this,

You are Chosen.

You are Royal.

You are Holy.

You are God's Special Possession.

You are Called out of darkness.

No matter your past choices or circumstances, no matter your present surroundings, you are who God says you are. Now that you've written it, say it out loud. It may sound kinda weird at first but keep saying it and put a little attitude on it. Because it's the truth! You are created on purpose for a purpose. God knew you would be where you are right now. He knew all the things you would face and go through in this life before making it to this particular moment.

I'm sure this journey called life may not have been easy. You might even be saying, "But you don't know what I've gone through" or maybe wondering, "If God knew, why did He let me go through that?" I want to remind you that God never intended or wanted you to ever hurt. He never wanted you to go through pain, but He knew that being here on this broken earth would bring pain and obstacles your way. He has also never left you and He never will. He has seen every tear, every scar, every silence and outcry for help. He hears you, He loves you and He cares about you.

David wrote in Psalm 56:8,

"You keep track of all my sorrows.
You have collected all my tears in your bottle.
You have recorded each one in your book."

In your quiet time, continue to read through verses 9-13 and you will see how David goes on to say that no matter what stood against Him, God was right there to rescue him, and because of that he could trust in God's promises—and we can too.

God prepared you for this journey, He has been

cheering you on, and has been right there for you this entire time. Even in the moments when you may have felt like you didn't hear Him and didn't see Him moving, He was still there. Stop for a moment, just quietly pause, take a deep breath in and let it out....

You are here right now. You are still breathing, no matter what's going on around you or what has happened to you, no matter what mistakes you've made. You are here right now, we are meeting together with Jesus through this book and His Word. Just pause where you are, and tell God, "I'm ready for MY next chapter." Just take a moment and thank Him for bringing you safely this far.

And even after reading this book, and praying all the prayers, you may not feel like you are all these things that God says about you. There may be days when so much has happened, and the days are so full of all the "to do's" and responsibilities, that you may not feel so Royal.

This, my friend, is when you find your grit. Grit is when you don't feel like you have it all together, but you bear down and make up your mind to get it together anyway.

Webster's definition of grit is "sharp granules of sand or gravel." We normally see that term when we buy sandpaper or nail files. There are different types of grit. Different surfaces and different projects need a different type and strength of grit. If you get the wrong grit, it can ruin the surface and take your project longer to complete. Grit is not something that you muster up in your own strength; grit is a determination to take God at His Word, in spite of how you feel.

So, when you feel like you just can't, or like your

back is up against the wall and you're overwhelmed, depleted, or just don't feel worthy, get your grit back, and determine in your spirit that what God says about you is true, regardless of how you feel. Get up, wash your face, take another deep breath in, let another deep breath out, and adjust your crown.

My friend, God's not done with you yet. Did you think it was over? No ma'am, He has GREAT things in store for you! And I'm not talking about the cliche, "God has a plan for you" type of stuff. No, God REALLY has a plan for YOU. It's been tailor-made just for YOU.

Ephesians 2:10 says,

"For we are God's <u>handiwork</u>, <u>created in Christ Jesus to do good works</u>, which God <u>prepared in advance</u> for us to do."

You see, He created you way in advance to do good works, and that plan has not changed.

Listen, you are created on purpose for a purpose. You are royalty, and nobody can fit the crown God made just for you. Nobody else could have made it through the things you've made it through. Nobody else could handle the way you've bounced back, after going down a dark path. Nobody has, or will ever have, the exact same journey as you.

That's why the new clothes **(yes girl, He gave you something new to wear and not the name your past called you)**, the crown, the anointing, the calling, the passion, and the purpose that God has for you. Nobody can wear it the way you do. You may already know your calling and purpose in this life. Or maybe you're in a season when you're just not sure what that is. Someone once told me, if you don't know what to do next, do the last thing God told you to do.

That may be to get up, wipe those tears, wash your face, look in the mirror and smile at the beautiful creation you are. It may be to stop worrying if you are a good mother, or if you'll ever be a mother at all. It may be to stop doubting that you could start that business or write that book. It might be to walk away from some toxic relationships and finally heal.

Whatever your next step may be, start with this...

Declaring that YOU ARE ROYALTY! You are worthy in the eyes of God. No amount of insecurity, worry, fear, mistakes, rejection, or abuse can steal that fact. YOU ARE WORTHY! As a daughter of the Most High King, you can take one step forward in confidence, knowing that God created you on purpose for a purpose.

Now, chile, in the words of my grandmother, it's time to hold your head high, adjust your crown, and strut yo stuff!

Chapter 5

Distractions...Devine Interruptions

**You *will keep in perfect peace all who trust in you,
all whose thoughts are fixed on you!*
Isaiah 26:3 NLT**

Distractions can be a purpose killer. We are living in the age when there are so many ways we can be distracted. There are over a million types of apps, tv shows, sporting events...not to mention just the normal day-to-day busy life: work, school, kids, kids activities, side hustles, relationships, bills. Distractions are anything that tries to shift our focus away from God.

There was a time when life was just stretched to the max for my husband and me. During the "years of growth," as we humorously like to refer to it, it felt like there were strains from every side, financially, emotionally, mentally, and physically—we felt drained, exhausted, and begin to struggle with our faith.

The "years of growth" was a period of two years when we lost two babies, lost our first house, and lost a lot of our close friends, all at the same time. We were starting to doubt our purpose and ourselves. We were even starting to doubt God. I personally was angry and hurt; all of these hurtful things were happening that most of the world was telling us we could control and fix by working harder or being better.

My prayers had turned to mostly nothing but ugly crying, while my heart was growing bitter by the day.

I wanted to know how we could we work harder and do better. What did these friends, colleagues, and family members mean by this? My husband worked two jobs. I also worked. We tithed. We worked at our marriage and regardless of the good and the bad, we tried to make God the center of it. We served in our church, we helped others whenever God asked, we were involved with our kids at school and on the field or on the basketball court. But these hurtful events were still happening. It felt like our best wasn't good enough.

Now, I'm not saying that we regret serving for the Kingdom of God in any capacity. And we loved seeing our kiddos dance and literally play ALL the sports. But have you ever felt like you were doing all the "right" things and yet still nothing is getting any better? You've prayed all the prayers and nothing has changed?

Sometimes we try to distract ourselves from the painful events in life by doing more "good things" such as serving in church or in the community, designing more Pinterest boards, or scrolling for hours on Facebook or the Gram, or taking our kids, to every after-school activity known to man. However, if we were to stop, breathe, and look closely, we can see all the little ways God may be trying to get our attention and give us hope.

Sometimes, we're so busy striving to do all the "good" things, and so busy listening to the voices that tell us to keep going, keep pushing through, that we don't hear God's voice clearly telling us to simply, BE STILL.

*"**Be still**, and **know** that I am God! I will be honored by every nation. I will be honored throughout the*

world." Psalm 46:10

God has a way of getting our attention. He has a way of getting us to still our hearts and minds until our focus and our honor is back on Him. The reason for this is because God does not desire to see His children so weighed down with the issues of this world, or so consumed with busyness that our peace is disturbed.

Jesus says in Matthew 11:28, "Come to me, all of you who are weary and carry heavy burdens, and I will give you rest."

God wants us to have peace—peace that only He can give.

And let's be real, it can be hard to release control. Especially as women, we do so much. We wear so many different hats. We wear the hats of a chef, nurse, doctor, counselor, chauffeur, butler, maid, handyman, and that's just on Monday! Let's not even get into the rest of the roles we fill, especially if we work full time jobs then have full time families, friends, or loved ones that we look after.

But when we are so busy striving, being stretched thin, and getting caught up in our list of "to-do's," we miss our opportunity to see our "get-to's." This is where God uses divine interruptions.

After feeling like we had experienced so much loss, God blessed us to conceive our baby boy. This was a joyous occasion, it should have been viewed as a rainbow in the midst of a storm, but I wasn't looking through the promise lens of God. Instead, I was looking at the storm and missing God's promise all together. I no longer wanted to pursue the things of God, I didn't talk to Him as much as I had before, I didn't have the desire to do anything. I had allowed the distractions to drain my energy and kill my drive for pursuing God's purpose and peace for my life.

We were facing hard times and trying so hard to put on a brave face as if everything were okay. We didn't want our children to worry. We even opened up with some of our friends about the things we were facing. What we heard in return was that we needed more faith, or to keep pressing through. How do you keep an engine going if it's running on fumes? By this time, I was definitely running on fumes. I'd ignored the cues from God to be still and just rest and heal. I'd even ignored the people God tried to use to tell me to come to Him and rest.

You see, when we are stretched thin, tired, and starting to feel confused with days running together, those are our red flags to sit still. God can't use us effectively to reflect Him when we're striving like that. He doesn't want us so busy that we're ignoring the issues of life that do come our way. And issues come sometimes, whether we want them to come or not. Trials don't need an invitation, they are the unwanted guests of the party. You know the ones, the trials that come to interrupt our agenda: The news that comes and hits you like a ton of bricks, making the world around you stop or go in slow motion, and those heart-sinking, gut-wrenching, unexpected moments.

When we are striving, we are no longer being genuine; we're performing. We're putting on a brave face, while inside we're crumbling to pieces or just plain tired.

When those hard-to-swallow moments happen, or even when your body is just yelling, "Chile, please sit down," we need to listen. Because when we surrender to God in those interruptions, we can hear His voice the clearest. We can hear Him leading us and comforting us.

In that season, where we were experiencing all of this hurt and loss at one time, there was this moment when I was home alone. Boxes were all packed up and stuff was everywhere. The kids were all at school, my husband was at work, and the plans I had to meet with a friend that day had fallen through. And there I was in this house where, for reasons beyond our control, we couldn't stay. I looked around and picked up my phone, only to see that it had gone dead. So, I sat there, trying to see if there was anything else that I could get done...when all I heard...was silence. Complete silence.

A silence that I had been avoiding for months, a silence that was so loud, it pierced my heart. There was absolutely nothing I could distract myself with this time. No errand to run, no one to meet with, no one to call. Just me and this silence.

Then it seemed, all at once, like the weight of everything we had gone through hit me like a punch to the gut. The loss of two babies, losing our home, losing close friends that we had loved and done life with for the past seven years. I began crying so hard, I couldn't breathe. I felt like the wind had been knocked out of me.

I felt God saying, "I'm here, daughter, now give it to Me." I didn't know how, I didn't want to look these things in the face. I didn't want to have to process it, I just wanted Him to take the pain away and make it all better again.

He said, "Surrender." I thought I knew what surrender looked like prior to this moment, but I only had a surface view before now.

This heartache hurt throughout my entire body. I didn't want to hurt like this. I had faced hard things before. A part of me sort of felt like, after all the things I'd gone through in my lifetime: rape, divorce, teen pregnancy, single motherhood, what I went through with my oldest son, and all sorts of health issues, that THIS shouldn't hurt as bad. THIS shouldn't cripple me like it was...but it did. And there I was, colliding with the truth that we are not immune. No matter all the "good" things we do, no matter how much we really do love the Lord, we are not immune to the trials and brokenness of this world. Sometimes, there are things that happen that are beyond our control, things that happen not because we did something wrong, or because we didn't do enough.

Jesus faced many challenges on this earth. He was despised, rejected, beaten, and bruised (Isaiah 53:5); doubted by loved ones (John 6:41- 42); betrayed by friends (Matthew 26:50); denied by some who walked close by Him (Matthew 26: 69-75); tempted (Mark 1:13); facing homelessness (Matthew 8:20), and He knew sorrow (Matthew 26:38). Even though He's fully God, He came to us wrapped in human flesh (John 1:14). That means He could feel. It means He does feel. And through everything He faced while here on earth, He didn't become immune to it. No, He still felt every agonizing blow until death (Acts 8:32), and He overcame it (Matthew 27:65-66).

We will never have to face anything more than what Jesus has faced. He went through all of this for us so that we would have a God who understands us, who sympathizes with us, and is there for us.

The Word says because of the joy that was set before Him, He endured the cross. (Hebrews 12:2) Death didn't bring Jesus joy, it was what was going to happen after His death that brought Him joy. When He conquered the grave on that third day, He rose with power in His hands and "sat at the right hand of the throne of God." (Hebrews 12:2) This is power that would be freely given to all of us (Luke 10:19), power to look the thing in the face—the thing that's trying to kill us, steal from us, or destroy us, and declare victory.

Facing trials isn't joyous. But after we've cried all the tears we can cry throughout the night, then joy comes in the morning. We discover a new day, a new beginning, a new strength that's found in connecting with Jesus.

My grandmother used to say, "If you don't have anything else to pray, just say His Name, Jesus. And if you don't have strength enough to say Jesus, just hum praises to Him." She said, "The devil doesn't understand praise." She would say that praise confuses the enemy, because "just when the devil thinks we should've been dead, we find new strength in our worship to the Father."

Whew, chile, that just gave me new breath right there! Worship does that. It has a way of centering our hearts on something higher than ourselves. It shifts our focus from how big our circumstances are, to how big our Father in Heaven is. God is bigger than your biggest problem.

Well, that day when I felt like the weight of all our trials was hitting me at once, I worshipped. At first, I did what my grandmother said, I hummed. I ugly cried and hummed. I rocked back and forth in the fetal position humming and crying. I started humming, "No other help I now," by Mahalia Jackson:

"When I've done all I can do,
When I've gone as far as I can go,
When I fall further right,
And grow weak in my fight,
Then I say Father I stretch my hand , my hand to thee
No other help, no other help I know"

(Hymn title: "Father, I Stretch my Hands to Thee," by Charles Wesley, circa 1740-60).

Then I started humming, "Reckless Love," by Stephanie Gretzinger:

"Before I spoke a word, You were singing over me
You have been so, so good to me
Before I took a breath, You breathed Your life in me
You have been so, so kind to me
Oh, the overwhelming, never-ending, reckless love
of God
Oh, it chases me down, fights 'til I'm found, leaves the
ninety-nine
I couldn't earn it, and I don't deserve it, still, You give
Yourself away
Oh, the overwhelming, never-ending, reckless love of
God.

(Reckless Love,© Caleb Culver, Cory Asbury, Ran Jackson; Bethel Music, Song ID 70319).

Then, I started to hum, "Gracefully Broken" by Tasha Cobbs Leonard:

"Take all I have in these hands and multiply
God, all that I am and find my heart
On the altar again set me on fire, set me on fire

Take all I have in these hands and multiply
God, all that I am and find my heart
On the altar again set me on fire, set me on fire
Here I am, God
Arms wide open
Pouring out my life
Gracefully broken."

(Gracefully Broken©, 2017; Matt Redman, Tasha Cobbs Leonard, et al., Digital Sheet Music).

By this time, I had gotten up off the floor laughing. I was standing with my arms outstretched towards Heaven and laughing. Meanwhile, my husband walked in the door, and saw me doing this. I looked over at him, and I thought, *he's probably thinking, 'what did I marry?* But again, I didn't care what it looked like. Without saying a word, I went right back to laughing, stretching my arms towards Heaven and praising Jesus. My husband didn't say a word to me, he just threw down the keys and joined me. We cried, laughed, prayed, and praised for hours.

I'm praying right now that God will surround you with His people. Hallelujah, I said, <u>His</u> people, who will not call you crazy, but will cry, laugh and get their Halal (crazy praise) on with you, people who are far from perfect, but have a love for Jesus that's unmatched.

I wasn't laughing because my circumstances had changed. I was laughing because after spending time in the presence of a faithful God, I had changed. I praise God for that day of silence. I love that God wants to get our attention and spend time with us. Since then, I've learned the three Ss of faith: Sit, Seek, and Surrender. When you're faced with something, <u>sit</u> down, <u>seek</u> the face of God, and <u>surrender</u> to His plans. I've also learned that even when we're not facing a trial, our family doesn't have to do ALL. THE. THINGS! Saying "no" is an act of worship too, honey!

Right now, take just a moment to sit and seek. Is there something that has been distracting you from focusing on God's purpose for your life? Write at least one thing you can say "no" to, just for this season, even if it's just saying no to social media for a week, so that you can seek more of God.

_____

_____

_____

_____

Now Surrender...

Surrender means to fully give oneself up into the power of another; it means fully letting go of what you're holding onto and releasing it into the hands of a faithful God. Surrendering is <u>fully</u> giving yourself to God.

Surrendering may first look like going to God because you need something from Him, but true surrender is going to God just to be with Him. Regardless of your agenda, or schedule, or problems, it means being with God because of who He is, not because of what He can do.

This next space is for you to do just that. What is it that you need to surrender to God today?

_____

_____

_____

Take some time today to just worship. Turn on some praise and worship music, or do what my grandmother said, just hum. Whatever it looks like for you, just sit, seek, and surrender.

Chapter 6

It's Vital

So then, just as you received Christ Jesus as Lord, continue to live your lives in him... **Colossians 2:6**

I had the privilege of being in the medical field for a little over 12 years. I used to love talking with the patients and helping them. No matter what each of them came in for, my goal was that when they left, no matter how they felt physically, they would each feel just a little touch of joy and peace. And the feisty ones were my favorites because I identify with them; I know when I don't feel well, I can be a WHOLE handful.

But when we go to the doctor, one of the first things that's usually checked is our vitals. Usually, before we're seen for whatever reason we came in for, our four main vitals are checked. They will sometimes check our blood pressure, heart rate, respiratory rate, and body temperature. But why? Why are our vitals checked first?

Because it's important. Now don't roll your face right here, hang with me for a minute. The word vital means, of the utmost importance. Our vitals are checked first because our vitals provide important information about what's going on in our body, <u>beneath the surface</u>.

If there is an illness or disease present, our vitals will almost always show this information. Our vitals can also help detect possible risk factors for other conditions. For example, high blood pressure could increase the risk of heart problems. The doctor uses our vitals to evaluate the best course of action for improving our overall health.

Our vitals are the body's way of shouting, "Help, something's wrong" or peacefully saying, "I'm good." The same way our vitals show the internal condition of our most vital organs, so it is also in our spiritual walk.

You see, our vitals in our spiritual walk are the evidence of how we are cooperating with the redemptive work of our Savior to reach the heart of God's people (blood pressure).

Colossians 2:6-7 says, "So then, just as you received Christ Jesus as Lord, continue to live your lives in Him, rooted and built up in him, strengthened in the faith, as you were taught, and overflowing with thankfulness."

In verse 8, Paul goes on to warn against being taken captive by "hollow and deceptive philosophies, which depend on human tradition and the elemental spiritual forces of this world rather than on Christ."

Jesus willingly laid down His life for us so that ALL could be reconciled to God (John 3:16). He didn't lay down His life and raise it back up again for our convenience and human rationale of what's good or normal, or for our human traditions. How we treat each other should not be based on what we look like, what our background is, or what financial status we have. Evidence of being a believer is not dressing the part or doing all the "good" things. The evidence of whom we believe in is shown when we're met with someone who doesn't look like us, talk like us, or walk like us. The evidence of whom we believe in is also shown when we encounter those whose views challenge the way we think. The evidence of who we view as Lord is shown when we pass a homeless person on the street and when we ignore the prompting of Holy Spirit to pray for that person who rubs us the wrong way.

2 Corinthians 5:15 says, "He died for everyone so that those who receive his new life will no longer live for themselves. Instead, they will live for Christ, who died and was raised for them."

What all of humanity has in common, whether we accept it or not, is the shed blood of a risen Savior who loves each of us so much that He was willing to cross all backgrounds and barriers of sin to reach each one of us. Jesus defied all laws of logic and nature just so He could show you how much He loves you and wants to use you to share His love with others.

He didn't die so we could have a shallow faith, one that only deals with the things that are on the surface and never going any deeper. Dealing with what's beneath the surface should be first so that we can be a body of believers who are "rooted and built up in Him, strengthened in the faith."

Our spiritual vitals are also the evidence of our compassion in the earth, how we love one another (heart rate).

Jesus said, "A new command I give you: Love one another. As I have loved you, so you must love one another. By this everyone will know that you are my disciples, if you love one another" (John 13:34-35).

The way that we love each other should match the heartbeat of Jesus Christ. His love meets each of us where we are and He loves us unconditionally. He doesn't love us so much that He overlooks our disobedience, and He doesn't love us too little, when He's completely disconnected and makes us work for His love. He exposes and extinguishes the sin, then loves and restores us.

Jesus says to the Pharisees in Matthew 12:33-35, "Make a tree good and its fruit will be good, or make a tree bad and its fruit will be bad, for a tree is recognized by its fruit...<u>For the mouth speaks what the heart is full of.</u> A good man brings good things out of the good stored up in him, and an evil man brings evil things out of the evil stored up in him."

Jesus also said in Matthew 5:8, "Blessed are the pure in heart, for they will see God." What we say is the fruit of what is planted in our hearts. So how can we align our hearts with the heartbeat of Jesus? By repenting (turning away) from sin, humbling ourselves and declaring we can't do it on our own, acknowledging that we desperately need Jesus, and by falling in love with the person of Jesus Christ by seeking Him through His Word and intimate worship.

Our spiritual vitals are also how we're stewarding the breath that God put inside our bodies (respiratory rate). Are we using His breath through our lungs to praise Him and build His Kingdom? Or are we using it to praise ourselves, and tear down others?

Isaiah 42:5 says, "...the Creator of the heavens, who stretches them out, who spreads out the earth with all that springs from it, who gives <u>breath</u> to its people, and <u>life</u> to those who walk on it."

Paul wrote in Acts 17:24- 25, "The God who made the world and everything in it is the Lord of the heaven and earth...He Himself gives everyone life and breath and everything else."

The Psalmist wrote, "Let everything that has breath praise the Lord. Praise the Lord." (Psalms 150:6)

Our breath is powerful, and I'm not just talking about first thing in the morning before the toothpaste works it's magic, either. Our breath has power because it was placed inside each of us, not by our own power or strength, but by the One True Living God. The same breath that God first breathed into the lungs of Adam is inside you.

With that same breath, God spoke the world into existence. So, when we speak, we are breathing out the creative power of God. When we speak, we're either advancing hell, or advancing the kingdom of God.

Satan loves when we speak negative words over ourselves, our lives, and others. He knows that when we speak the Word of God over our lives, faith that God is who He says He is, is released and mountains are moved. (Mark 11:23)

Proverbs 18:21 says, "The tongue has the power of life and death..."

James broke it down how the tongue behaves, in James 3:2-12:

"Indeed, we all make many mistakes. For if we could control our tongues, we would be
perfect and could also control ourselves in every other way.
We can make a large horse go wherever we want by means of a small bit in its mouth.
And a small rudder makes a huge ship turn wherever the pilot chooses to go,

even though the winds are strong.
In the same way, the tongue is a small thing that makes grand speeches.
But a tiny spark can set a great forest on fire.
And among all the parts of the body, the tongue is a flame of fire.
It is a whole world of wickedness, corrupting your entire body.
It can set your whole life on fire, for it is set on fire by hell itself.
People can tame all kinds of animals, birds, reptiles, and fish, but no one can tame the tongue.
It is restless and evil, full of deadly poison.
Sometimes it praises our Lord and Father, and sometimes it curses those who have been made in the image of God.
And so blessing and cursing come pouring out of the same mouth.
Surely, my brothers and sisters, this is not right!
Does a spring of water bubble out with both fresh water and bitter water? Does a fig tree produce olives, or a grapevine produce figs?
No, and you can't draw fresh water from a salty spring."

We can steward the breath of God by getting control over our mouths and refusing to speak anything but the Word of God over our lives and situations. Above all else, we can "guard our hearts, because out of it, flow the issues of life." (Proverbs 4:23)

What a privilege we have, to steward the breath of God! God didn't leave us in a broken world hopeless and helpless. Not only did He give us power and authority through His son Jesus, but He gave us His creative power, through what we speak.

Matthew 12:36 says that on the day of judgement, we will give an account for every careless word we speak.

Why would we have to give an account for every careless word we speak? Because God equipped us with His breath to breathe life back into the world—to bring Heaven to earth with every word.

Right now, in the name of Jesus Christ, declare over yourself that with every breath you breathe out, you will now build the Kingdom of Heaven. Declare, from this day forward, that you will let no corrupt communication proceed out of your mouth, but only that which is good for building up, and bring grace to those who listen (Ephesians 4:29).

Whew, chile, God ain't playing with us about these vitals! He wants us to be healed and whole from the inside out.

Let's review real quick: Our spiritual vitals are the evidence of how we cooperate with the redemptive work of our Savior to reach the heart of God's people (blood pressure); the evidence of our compassion in the earth through how we love one another (heart rate); how we're stewarding the breath that God put inside our bodies (respiratory rate), and it's also the temperature at which we're choosing to operate in our faith.

Are we lukewarm, going through the motions and doing the bare minimum? Or are we on fire for Jesus, running fearlessly after Him, and sharing who He is every chance we get?

Jesus said in Revelation 3:15-16, "I know all the things you do, that you are neither hot nor cold. I wish that you were one or the other! But since you are like lukewarm water, neither hot nor cold, I will spit you out of my mouth!"

Can you imagine, on a freezing cold day, going to a coffee shop to grab a hot chocolate or some hot beverage, and you can't wait to take that first careful sip? You can picture how good it will feel as you sip it and it begins to warm your entire body. Except when you get it, and you take that first sip, it's not hot or cold, it's just...meh. It doesn't warm your body at all. The taste is not even as expected. It's called HOT chocolate...not lukewarm chocolate. There's usually HOT tea, or ICED tea, not lukewarm tea.

It would also be the same if you wanted a cold drink on a scorching hot day. Beads of sweat running down your face, your mouth is dry, and you're thirsty beyond words. You run in the house, open the fridge, and pull out a sports drink that you know should be cold and ready for you to chug down. Only, when you open it and begin to drink, it's lukewarm. It's as if you left it sitting out on the counter all day.

Now, I do have to stop right here, because I know some good people who love lukewarm drinks. They don't like their drinks piping hot, and they don't like their water, juice, or sports drinks in the refrigerator. No judgement, okay, sisters? We just won't ask you to bring the beverages to our next gathering, okay? Just kidding!

But seriously, the same way that some of us would prefer our hot drinks to be hot, and our cold drinks to be cold, God would rather us be ALL in, or not in at all. We seem to live in a no-effort culture, where companies' marketing strategies include making sure the customer doesn't have to put in a lot of effort, time, or money. Hey, and as a busy mom of five, I appreciate companies that want to save me time and money. But consumer hazard comes when we start thinking we are not to be inconvenienced in any way. We can't wait more than two days for an item to arrive that we ordered offline. If we missed a sale, we want to call companies and raise sand and berate into tears the customer service associate, who's just trying to put food on their table, until they give in and give us the sale price or some sort of compensation for the inconvenience of our missing a sale.

I remember the good old days, where if you missed a sale, you missed a sale. We didn't blame the store because we missed it. When we went inside the store, and something was out of stock, it was just out of stock, or we would go to a different store.

This no-effort, right now culture cannot be applied to our faith. We might pray today, and there is no guaranteed money back or two-day shipping on an answered prayer. The temperature of our faith is displayed when things aren't easy, or don't go exactly as we had planned.

My grandmother used to say, "When you put a teabag in hot water, its true colors will come out." What she meant was when we are placed in the uncomfortable pressures of life, that's when it shows whether we've been in a relationship with Jesus, or whether we've been going through the motions.

You see, going to church, reading your devotion, reading a verse a day to keep the devil away, don't help when you're in the hot waters of life. When you immerse a tea bag into piping hot water, the contents of the teabag remain intact. They remain intact because they are <u>sealed</u> in a small porous bag. That bag was specifically designed only to let the vibrant colors and flavors of the tea seep out into the cup of water.

When we are no longer going through the motions, and we make the intentional effort to go deeper in our relationship with God, we know - that we know - that we know - that we know - that without a shadow of a doubt, we are sealed in the love of His shed blood. So, when stuff gets hot, when the trials of life get so uncomfortable and almost unbearable, the only thing overflowing from our hearts, our mouths, and our actions is Jesus.

There's another quality about that tea bag; the longer you let the tea bag sit in the hot water, the stronger it gets. There are some things the Lord can't get out of you, until you sit in that hot uncomfortable place for a while. It's the place of humility, where we are no longer able to strive within ourselves to "look the part" or play the role of "perfect Christian." It's the place of breaking where, while we're going through that situation, we are stripped of all pride and we experience a breakthrough like never before. He wants to show you just how strong He is through you. He wants to display His power and strength in your vulnerability.

Oftentimes, we don't like or want to be in those hot situations and will even beg God to please pull us out. We don't stay there forever, but we stay there long enough, until a complete surrender takes place when we're ready to let go of trying to control and tell God we trust Him.

Let's make sure we put this in the correct lens. This isn't God standing over us, watching us suffer. No, this is a loving Father wanting to help His daughter carry things that are too weighty, too heavy, and too strenuous for her to carry. But every time He tries to help,

His daughter slaps His hands away, and stubbornly says, "I got it."

Women, we are not helpless; on the contrary, we are strong. But we are only strong through the power of God. It can get tiring and exhausting when we try to carry the weights of this life on our own. Trying to handle all the issues of life, be everyone's everything all the time, is too much for our shoulders to carry. That's why we need to stay ever dependent on a Heavenly Father who could very well display His power apart from us. Yet He <u>chooses</u> to display His power <u>through</u> us.

When Paul asked God to remove a thorn from his side, God said, "My grace is sufficient for you, for my power is made perfect in weakness." (2 Corinthians 12:9) God wants to display His power through your transparency, and His willingness to be <u>real</u> in the earth.

God doesn't force Himself on us. With each one of my children, I can remember when they first started to walk. At first, they had to hold our hand, or hold on to something to keep their balance as they learned how to make each step. But they eventually got to this stage where we didn't have to hold their hand the entire time. My husband or I would maybe help them stand up, or maybe hold their hand for the first few steps just to get them started, then gently let go and watch them continue to waddle down the hallway. Once they got a little more confident, and a little bit older, we would try to hold their hand and they would snatch it back and take off running.

This was so cute because that's the picture of our little one becoming independent. But even though they were becoming more independent, there were times when they still needed to hold our hands, whether they wanted to or not. For example, crossing the street. If we didn't hold their hands when they were toddlers crossing the street, they would have taken off running into oncoming traffic. Holding our hands was for their protection.

Even as years go by and they are no longer toddlers, but teenagers, there are still those tough moments when they're in those hot water situations, but they want to be independent and tell us they don't want our help. They want to prove that they can do it themselves. We don't force our help on them. Instead, we let them recognize on their own that they need help. Because after they're done striving, they begin to realize that even though they can do it by themselves, it would be so much easier if they had help. In those moments, they realize, "I can't do this by myself," and they come to my husband or me and we would hold their hands and help them through whatever they need.

God knows that you were built to be strong and independent because He made you. You were created in His image and likeness. But, daughter, there are some hot situations when you need your Heavenly Father to hold your hand all the way through, to love you in the right way and to show you that you don't have to struggle alone.

Some of us, for whatever reason, may have tension with the idea of being dependent on someone else, especially if you say, "Father." Maybe you had an earthly father who passed away too soon, or maybe one who abused his role in your life, or abused your mom, or maybe wasn't there at all. But let me tell you right now, you have a Heavenly Father who has been here all along. He's been waiting for you to reach out and hold His hand. This Father will not harm you or leave you.

He wants to heal the damage that was done to you, woman of God. You are not damaged goods; you are not fatherless. You have a Heavenly Father who loves you so much, with a Holy love for which He gave His life as a ransom through His Son, Jesus Christ. He knew that you would have a hard time trusting Him, so He made the first move of dying for you. He wanted you to know that His love is not harmful, or absent; it's not prideful or insecure. He wanted you to know that His love is safe. There's nothing you nor I can do to ever earn or discount ourselves from this holy, unconditional love. He knows your heart and knows what you've been through, and He made a decision before you were born to love you anyway.

We don't deserve this type of love, but because of Jesus' sacrifice on the cross and arising at the grave, we are deserving. We don't have to hold His hand. We don't have to be dependent on Him. But, <u>we get to</u>. It's an opportunity to rest. This may sound crazy, but when we are in those hot situations of life, those situations when those bills are piling up, that paycheck doesn't stretch far enough, there's a to-do list that's longer than the daylight offered, people are walking out of your life, the children are going crazy, you face demands on the job, and there's stress on every side, it's an opportunity to rest. We must accept God's invitation to rest, especially in those hot situations that tend to thrust us face-to-face with our insecurities, our trust issues, and our pride.

I don't know about you, but those are the moments when I desperately need a Father, a Daddy who comes through just in the nick of time. God is THE Father who steps in, while my head is down and I'm filled with feelings of unworthiness, or faced with the lie of insecurity, just to tell me truth. He'll come to tell me that

He built me worthy and worth loving. He encourages me by telling me "that battle you're trying to fight, it's not yours, it's Mine." (2 Chronicles 20:15) He's a Father who says, "I know they hurt you, but vengeance is Mine." (Romans 12:19) "I know they told you that you wouldn't be anything, but daughter with Me, you can do anything." (Philippians 4:13) He's a Father who cries with us (Psalm 34:18), then gets up fighting on our behalf (Exodus 14:14). He's also a Father who comes back from battling our enemies and hands the victory over into our hands for us to claim as our own. (2 Chronicles 20:17)

That's the type of Heavenly Father we have. He also wants more for us, more than just us going through the motions. When we spend time with Him, that goes beyond going through the motions and checking off our Christian to do list: Church ✔ Bible Study ✔ verse a day ✔. And we begin to go deeper in our relationship with Him, when we no longer want anything from Him, but just want to get to know Him, when we are no longer seeking His hand, but seeking His heart, that's when we find a very REAL God. (Jeremiah 29:13) That's when the evidence of His love and power will be displayed in how we live, breathe, and move. (Acts 17:28)

No matter where you are in your faith journey, whether you just started, or you're 50 seasons in, let's take a moment together and get quiet with God. Get still—no striving, no pretending— and just allow God right now to fill you with His peace and to show you His love.

I want to take a moment and pray for you, my sweet sister:

Father God, right now in the name of Jesus, I lift my

sister up to You. Only You know what's in her heart. Only You know what she stands in need of. Lord release Your power and fill my sister with a peace that goes beyond understanding. Miracles happen when You move and healing comes when You enter the room. Lord, right now we are expectant that a right now healing is taking place in my sister, that miracle she's been praying for is about to break loose right now. By the authority You've given us through Christ Jesus, I declare that the woman reading this right now is being restored, revived, and healed from the crown of her head to the soles of her feet. That right now, a surrender is happening in her spirit, to release control and trust You to do exactly what You promised. You call her daughter, chosen, holy, royal, and a joint heir with Christ Jesus. Her inheritance of abundance is being released over her right now, Lord, and when my sister gets up from spending time with You, may she feel brand new. May she never be the same after being with You. From this moment forward, may she get real with You so that You can show just how real and good You are. In the name of Jesus, with her arms wide open, and her heart ready for You to pour out more of Your love, fill her with more of who You are. After this moment of being still with You, may she know that she is loved and worthy. In Your holy and matchless name, Jesus, I pray, Amen.

Today, take time to rest in Him because your dependence on Him is vital.

Jesus said in John 15:5, "I am the vine; you are the branches. If you remain in me and I in you, you will bear much fruit; apart from me you can do nothing." Then in verses 7 and 8, He says, "If you remain in me, and my words remain in you, ask whatever you wish, and it will be done for you. This is to my Father's glory, that you bear much fruit, showing yourselves to be my disciples."

Remaining with Jesus is not easy when life gets hard, but it's vital. It's necessary for spiritual survival. Growing deeper in your faith is a decision that you won't regret, because when the storms of life get hard, it's going to be well worth it for you to be deeply rooted in His love.

My prayer for you is what Paul prayed in Ephesians 3:16-19: "I pray that from his glorious, unlimited resources He will empower you with inner strength through His Spirit. Then Christ will make His home in your hearts as you trust in Him. Your roots will grow down into God's love and keep you strong. And may you have the power to understand, as all God's people should, how wide, how long, how high, and how deep His love is. May you experience the love of Christ, though it is too great to understand fully. Then you will be made complete with all the fullness of life and power that comes from God."

Chapter 7

Victory on the Table

*No, despite all these things, overwhelming victory
is ours through Christ, who loved us.*
Romans 8:37

L isten, my family loves food. If we don't do anything else, when we get together, we're gonna laugh and eat good. The men and women in my family also love cooking and feeding other people. My grandmother used to cook for everybody in the neighborhood. You could smell her stove heating up something good for miles down the road. Anybody who came by knew my grandmother would feed them. Neighbors, family from out of state, people passing through our state headed home, homeless people walking the street, everyone knew, if they went by to see "Annie Girl," as they liked to call her, she would feed them a hot meal, share some of her straight to the point wisdom, and send them on their way.

One of my grandmother's rules was you couldn't get up from the table until you finished all your food. That wasn't a problem for the adults, but for us, when we were kids, that was tough, especially if she made a vegetable we didn't want to eat. She would tell us, "You can't leave the table until you eat all of your food, it's good for you, and when someone makes you a good meal, you don't just leave it on the table."

And if you were just determined to sit there and not eat your vegetables, she would wrap your plate up, put it in the oven and say, "If you get hungry, your plate is in the stove." That was her not-so-subtle way of telling us kids that we weren't going to get a snack, or anything else, until we ate the food that was on that plate. She did not believe in wasting food. There was no getting a ton of snacks when we were growing up; we were going to eat the good food that Grandma put on the table.

If we all stop and think about it, there were some things that might have been put on our table, whether by family members, past choices, or past relationships, that we didn't ask for. There may have been some generational stuff like alcoholism, adultery, depression, anxiety, diabetes, cancer, poverty, divorce, teen pregnancy, you name it.

But no matter what the table of life has served you, dysfunction is not your legacy. There is victory on the table.

When you go to the doctor, they like to ask for your family history. This is supposed to give them an idea of what you may be genetically pre-disposed for. And it doesn't matter if you don't currently have these conditions, they want to know so they can watch and wait for those traits to manifest within you, and begin early treatment. In spite of any dysfunction or generational stuff being put on our table, there's something else that our Savior put on the table... Victory.

Romans 8: 37 says, "No, despite all these things, overwhelming victory is ours through Christ, who loved us."

Jesus is watching and waiting for this trait of victory to manifest itself within you. Early treatment begins when you accept it and enforce it.

Jesus took all our wounds, sicknesses, sins, mistakes, and nailed them to the cross. He told everything that was sent ahead of you to kill you, to stay back, when He rose up out of the grave on that third day. He came destroying every ounce of death and darkness that would ever think to cross your path (1 Corinthians 15:55-57). Then, He cooked up a good hot meal of victory, prepared the table for you, in front of your enemies, then said, "Here, daughter, feast on a victory that you didn't have to cook up yourself. It will fill you up, and you will lack nothing, and when I send you on your way, you will want to tell everyone about this one-of-a-kind home cooked meal."

The Psalmist (Psalm 23) David said it like this:

"The Lord is my shepherd, I lack nothing.
He makes me lie down in green pastures,
He leads me beside quiet waters, he refreshes my soul.
He guides me along the right paths for His name's sake.
Even though I walk through the darkest valley,
I will fear no evil,
For you are with me;
Your rod and your staff, they comfort me.
You prepare a table before me
In the presence of my enemies.
You anoint my head with oil;
My cup overflows.
Surely your goodness and love will follow me
All the days of my life,
and I will dwell in the house of the Lord forever."

The Lord is a good shepherd, He knows how to lead us and nourish us. In spite of what it looks like and the odds stacked against us, He anoints us and overflows our cup with blessings so we can be a blessing to someone else. There may have been some things that were done before you got here, and put on the table that made you pre-inclined to take it on yourself. You might have just thought, "Well, my whole family is like that, so I can't help it," or "My mother was a worrier, so I'm a worrier, too," or "This is genetic." But I declare in the Name of Jesus that all generational curses and sickness be broken off of you today!

I declare, right now, over you, sister, that dysfunction does not have to be your legacy. That <u>Victory</u> is NOW on the table!

Lies of insecurity, hopelessness, and unworthiness, you have to leave and break off of my sister right now, in the name of Jesus. Curses of rejection, poverty, sickness, divorce, you have no right and no place in my sister's life in Jesus Name. Everything that is contrary to the Word and will of God is trespassing and has to leave and be broken off of you right now!

Hallelujah! Thank You, Jesus, that this woman of God is sealed in Your shed blood, and seated at the right hand of the Father with You. She's seated with Jesus, with Victory on the table!

You may have been born into the dysfunction, married into it, or created it yourself, but it does not have to be your destiny or your identity; there is hope. You no longer have to eat what was passed down to you generationally. Jesus came and destroyed all generational curses and put victory on the table.

So now, you have a choice...there's Victory on the table. And when someone makes you a good meal, you don't just leave it on the table.

Grab hold of your victory and walk boldly into your next chapter.

Chapter 8

New Beginning

Forget about what's happened; don't keep going over old history. Be alert, be present. I'm about to do something brand-new. It's bursting out! Don't you see it? Isaiah 43:19 (MSG)

How God speaks to you is as different as each person's fingerprints. The way God speaks to you may not look like how He speaks to me, or your neighbor or friend. He wants to do a new thing through you.

Now, it's time for you to move into your season of expectancy. A season to take God at His Word and walk in your purpose. You are no longer a slave to fear and shame, because He calls you a child of God (Galatians 4:7).

There are many species of animals and insects that go through a life cycle called *metamorphosis*. Metamorphosis comes from the Greek word **Metamorphoó**, which means to transform. **Metamorphoó** comes from the root word **metá**. **Metá** means "to change after being with."

The butterfly is one species of insect that goes through metamorphosis and transforms from the inside out into something completely different and beautiful. A butterfly does not begin its journey as a butterfly. It begins its journey as a caterpillar. According to *The Academy of Natural Sciences of Drexel University,* after the egg stage of the butterfly's life cycle, the next stage is the larva or caterpillar. "The job of the caterpillar is to eat and eat and eat. As the caterpillar grows, it splits its skin and sheds about 4 or 5 times. Food eaten in this stage, is stored and used later as an adult. Caterpillars can grow 100 times their size during this stage." (https://ansp.org/)

After the caterpillar stage is the pupa, or chrysalis, or transition stage. In this stage, the caterpillar suspends itself under a branch and then begins to shed its skin to reveal the chrysalis forming within it. Once the chrysalis is fully revealed, the caterpillar begins its most gruesome, yet delicate stage of transformation.

While the caterpillar is inside the chrysalis, the tissues that make up the caterpillar begin to rearrange to form a butterfly. The chrysalis protects the caterpillar as it begins to transform. According to an article entitled, *Here's What Happens Inside a Caterpillar's Chrysalis,* written by Anthony Bouchard, "The caterpillar's body begins to release enzymes that dissolve cells in the insect's muscles and organs, leaving behind only the most vital life supporting cells."

The process of the caterpillar turning into a butterfly inside the chrysalis can take anywhere from a few weeks to a few months or years. The length of time it takes all depends on the butterfly's genes and climate. When the butterfly finally emerges, it leaves behind a "gooey fluid-like substance." "This substance is the waste that was produced during the transformation process." Also, when the butterfly emerges you can see the intricate details and colors of a beautiful creation. It emerges and spreads its wings and flies off to find another butterfly to partner with to start the whole process over again.

Caterpillars are born with everything they need to become butterflies.

Each butterfly has its own unique look, as well. There are hundreds of species of butterflies and all of them look different. And each individual butterfly has an intricate, unique wing pattern of colors. To us, it may look like someone took a tiny paintbrush and painted an abstract picture on the butterfly's wings. But what looks like a beautiful, abstract pattern to us is an intricately planned design that was strategically placed and woven on purpose.

When you walk in your calling, God calls forth the purpose that He instilled in you from the beginning. To some, we might look like an abstract painting or a beautiful hot mess, but what they don't see, is that when we were in the secret place with our Heavenly Father, He strategically imprinted His design on us.

Before you were born, He gave you everything you needed to become the woman that He designed you to be. You might have had to go through some life altering processes that caused you to be turned upside down and inside out, but when you emerge, it will be evident that God's hand was upon you.

It will look like you should not have survived what you went through. It will look like your survival odds were slim to none and close to impossible. It might have looked like you were hanging on by a slim thread attached to a branch, that should have broken when the winds of life blew your way. But all that you went through was so that you could emerge as something brand new, hand-crafted by God Himself. You're not coming out the way you went in.

The caterpillar's functions are completely different than the functions of a butterfly, even though they are the same. When the butterfly is in the beginning stage of being a caterpillar, its job is just to get nourishment and grow. When the caterpillar is in transition phase, its job is to be still and let what was placed on the inside of it come forth. When it emerges as a butterfly, its job is to fly and partner. It also goes on to provide a wide range of environmental benefits such as pollination and natural pest control.

Each stage of the butterfly's development is vital. It's not just beneficial for the butterfly to go through this process, but for all those around it. Yes, the butterfly emerges as this beautiful new creature, but it also plays an important part in the flourishing and development of the environment.

When you begin your journey with Jesus and begin to grow deeper in your relationship with Him, what God placed on the inside of you from the beginning begins to be birthed. There may be moments when it may not look pretty, and that's all everyone sees. In this process, God does not only call forth the purpose He placed on the inside you, but He also reveals the things that are not like Him (sin) that you can't take with you into the next stage.

First Peter 2 tells us that in order to grow in maturity of our faith, we must rid ourselves of "all malice, and all deceit, hypocrisy, envy, and slander of every kind. Like newborn babies, crave pure spiritual milk, so that by it you may grow up in your salvation, now that you have tasted that the Lord is good."

This ridding ourselves happens in our chrysalis

stage. When we are wrapped up in the Word of God and get still with Him, Holy Spirit begins to show us all the things that are not vital to our growth. Those things that God exposes in our hearts that don't look like Him, we leave behind, in order to grow into mature believers.

While you go deeper and deeper in your relationship with Him through sitting, seeking, and surrendering, God wraps you in His protective love. He tells all of hell to step back and back off, because, "My daughter is going through a breaking season. And when she comes out, she's gonna look like My glory. She's gonna have a new name, new clothes, and emerge as My royal heir, ready to spread My love throughout the earth."

Your money doesn't determine your calling, your past doesn't determine your calling, where or how you grew up doesn't determine your calling, only the One who deposited the calling inside of you in the first place can determine your calling.

The caterpillar doesn't stop and question God before it starts its journey of transformation. It doesn't look around and say, "Why can't I be like the bird? It just hatches straight from the egg, and after a while it learns to fly." The caterpillar doesn't complain and say, "Well, why do I have to put in all of this work? Working and then dying to myself, in order to finally turn into something that's beautiful." The caterpillar doesn't quit when it gets too hard, or say, "Whew, chile, this is too much! I think I'd rather just chill for a little bit!"

No, the caterpillar begins its journey with this stirring within itself that it knows what it's supposed to do. It does not get distracted, but instead stays focused on the journey. It does not get puffed up with pride, wanting to be more before its time. The caterpillar knows that if it focuses during the seasons of growth, there is going to come a day when it will be able to fly around and smell the roses. There will come a day when all the hard work and complete surrender will be well worth it. As you've learned, the butterfly's journey isn't over once it emerges from the chrysalis; it goes forth to find another butterfly to partner with in order to multiply and start the process all over again.

Our journey isn't over when we experience breakthrough. It is only the beginning. Now we are to partner with God and other believers to bring others into the Kingdom of Heaven.

> *"And I am sure of this, that He who began a good work in you will bring it to completion at the day of Jesus Christ."* (Philippians 1:6)

I don't know what stage you might be in right now. Maybe you have just started this journey with Jesus. Maybe this is your season to eat and eat more of the Word of God and grow fervently in your faith. Or maybe you've been on this journey a while. Maybe this is your season of being gracefully broken and being still in God's presence so that He can build you again. Or maybe this is the season when you've gone through all of those stages and are on the verge of your breakthrough. Whatever season you find yourself in, woman of God, now is not the season to get distracted or caught up in comparison or lies of insecurity.

This is your season of a new beginning. This is your season, woman of God, to wave the blood-stained banner of victory above sickness, defeat, insecurity, fear, and doubt. You have been made new through the sacrifice of Jesus Christ. You are equipped with His Word to enforce Heaven on earth. There is nothing you can't do when you stay connected to Jesus.

So, when the enemy tries to whisper "what it looks like" to you, claim your authority as a blood-bought child of God and declare what it really is, according to what God said in His Word. Declare what it will be according to the authority of Heaven and the Word of God!

The tears you shed and the pressures you went through were not all for nothing. God wastes nothing (John 6:12).

All of this is, "so that you will walk in a manner worthy of the Lord [displaying admirable character, moral courage, and personal integrity], to [fully] please Him in all things, bearing fruit in every good work and steadily growing in the knowledge of God [with deeper faith, clearer insight and fervent love for His precepts]; [we pray that you may be] strengthened and invigorated with all power, according to His glorious might, to attain every kind of endurance and patience with joy..." (Colossians 1:10-11)

No matter how many times you've fallen, or how battered and bruised you may feel, the enemy is not getting away with it this time. I declare that right now, where the enemy had success before, he will not succeed again (Nahum 1:9).

Let the Word of God be breathed out upon you right now. God is doing a new thing in your life! This next chapter is going to be greater than your last chapter. So, grab your sword (The Word of God), Turn the page, and write your story of victory!

Chapter 9

Your New Chapter

Then the LORD said to me, 'Write my answer plainly on tablets, so that a runner can carry the correct message to others.' **Habakuk 2:2**

This last chapter is for you to write. Write down what you believe God is saying to you regarding your next steps. Write down what you believe your God-given purpose is, and how you plan to use that purpose to tell others about the love of Jesus.

_____

_____

_____

_____

_____

_____

_____

_____

_____

_____

_____

_____

_____

_____

_____

_____

_____

Dear friend, my prayer is that through this book you have been encouraged and can clearly see your identity through the Word of God. I want you to know that God loves you. You are not defined by what you do, or where you've been. You have been given the name of daughter by our Heavenly Father. You are a joint-heir with Jesus Christ. You are Royalty.

Thank you for being brave enough to take this journey with me. Together we've uncovered the truth of what God says about us. I may not know you personally, but I feel like I do. We are sisters in faith. I am on this journey with you and God, as well. And I believe that God has greater things in store for us...a greater calling, a greater purpose. One thing is for certain, His great love is with us and will never leave us. No matter what we face ahead, we have a crown on our heads, and a sword in our hands (The Word of God) and will get through it Victoriously!

May "The Lord bless you and keep you; the Lord make his face shine on you and be gracious to you; the Lord turn His face toward you and give you peace." Numbers 6:24 -26

ABOUT
KHARIS PUBLISHING

KHARIS PUBLISHING is an independent, traditional publishing house with a core mission to publish impactful books, and channel proceeds into establishing mini-libraries or resource centers for orphanages in developing countries, so these kids will learn to read, dream, and grow. Every time you purchase a book from Kharis Publishing or partner as an author, you are helping give these kids an amazing opportunity to read, dream, and grow. Kharis Publishing is an imprint of Kharis Media LLC. Learn more at https://www.kharispublishing.com.